All About Dogs

West Highland White Terriers

Joy Gregory

AV2

www.openlightbox.com

AV2

Step 1
Go to **www.openlightbox.com**

Step 2
Enter this unique code
BZAYFLNR2

Step 3
Explore your interactive eBook!

AV2 is optimized for use on any device

Your interactive eBook comes with...

Contents
Browse a live contents page to easily navigate through resources

Audio
Listen to sections of the book read aloud

Videos
Watch informative video clips

Weblinks
Gain additional information for research

Slideshows
View images and captions

Try This!
Complete activities and hands-on experiments

Key Words
Study vocabulary, and complete a matching word activity

Quizzes
Test your knowledge

Share
Share titles within your Learning Management System (LMS) or Library Circulation System

Citation
Create bibliographical references following APA, CMOS, and MLA styles

This title is part of our AV2 digital subscription

1-Year K–5 Subscription
ISBN 978-1-7911-3320-7

Access hundreds of AV2 titles with our digital subscription.
Sign up for a FREE trial at **www.openlightbox.com/trial**

The digital components of this book are guaranteed to stay active for at least five years from the date of publication.

All About Dogs

West Highland White Terriers

Contents

Name That Dog

Which dog has a carrot-shaped tail?

Which dog tilts its head when it is interested in something?

What kind of dog is used to hunt rodents?

Which dog always has a white coat?

Did you guess the West Highland white terrier?

You are right!

West Highland White Terrier History

Hundreds of years ago, farmers in Great Britain kept small dogs. These dogs spent much of their time outside with the farmers. Many of the dogs were from **breeds** known as **terriers**.

In the 1700s, the Malcolm family began to breed white terriers in Scotland. Some people called the white dogs Poltalloch terriers. The name came from the Malcolm family home, the Poltalloch estate.

Scotland is on the island of Great Britain, to the north of the European continent. Along with England, Wales, and Northern Ireland, Scotland is part of the United Kingdom.

In 1907, a dog show in England exhibited one of these white terriers. The American Kennel Club (AKC), an organization that **registers** dog breeds in the United States, accepted the breed the following year. At first, it was registered as the Roseneath terrier. However, in 1909, the AKC changed the breed's name. Since then, these dogs have been called West Highland white terriers.

West Highland white terriers, or Westies, were bred to be working dogs. They helped farmers and hunters locate small animals. West Highland terriers are small, smart, and fast. In Scotland, hunters used them to corner burrowing animals. If the **prey** ran down a hole, the Westie would bark to get the hunter's attention. Then, it would hunt down the animal in the hole.

In 2022, the AKC ranked Westies as the 45th most popular dog breed in the United States.

Some terrier breeds are hard to spot in the field. Their **coats** blend in with nature and resemble those of animals that people may be hunting, such as foxes. Westies, with their white coats, are easier to see. When Westies were first bred, hunters liked knowing where their dogs were and being able to tell them apart from other animals.

A Westie's outer coat is about 2 inches (5 cm) long.

What They Look Like

The West Highland terrier is a small dog with short legs. Males stand 11 inches (28 centimeters) tall at the shoulder. They are slightly taller than females, who stand about 10 inches (25 cm) tall. Westies weigh 15 to 21 pounds (7 to 9.5 kilograms). Males are a little heavier than females.

Westies have a double coat of white fur that keeps them warm. A Westie's outer coat is stiff and wiry. It keeps the softer, shorter undercoat from getting wet or dirty.

Westies have a short tail that is shaped like a carrot. It curves toward the dog's back.

The bullet-like shape of a Westie's body helps it enter into the burrows and dens of small animals.

Westies have round heads that are slightly dome-shaped on top. Their eyebrows are heavy, with long and thick hair, and sit above small eyes and a black nose. The hair on their tails is flat and smooth. Westie legs are covered with thick, short hair.

A Westie's ears are located on the outer edge of its skull. The ears are shaped like pointed triangles. They stand straight up and face the same direction as the dog's eyes. The ears tip forward when these dogs are interested in what is happening. At the same time, Westies often tilt their heads to one side. When a Westie is relaxed and friendly, its ears tip back.

A Westie's dark brown eyes are shaped like almonds.

The Westie Personality

West Highland white terriers are high-energy dogs. They like to run, and can be taught to play games. Many Westies enjoy searching for items that their owners have hidden. They often wag their tails and bark to get attention.

Westies are always on the alert. These terriers tend to warn their owners of possible danger. When they see or hear a stranger or something new, they bark. This **trait** makes them good watchdogs.

Although Westies may be quite vocal, they can be trained to bark just once to alert their owners of something new.

A fence that is at least 3 feet (1 meter) high will keep a Westie in a yard. Westies enjoy digging, so objects should be placed along the bottom of a fence to make it harder for the dog to dig underneath.

Westies can be trained to live with a variety of other pets, including cats.

Westies like to be around people they know. They enjoy taking part in activities that make their owners happy. Westies are good with children and will snuggle up to the people they like the best. They often get along with other dogs, but do not typically like to share their toys.

These little dogs adapt well to a variety of living situations. Westies should be given the opportunity to spend time outdoors. Even though Westies enjoy outdoor exercise, they do not need a regular schedule. A Westie only needs about one hour of exercise each day. Many of these dogs are happy living in small homes and apartments.

Westie Puppies

West Highland white terrier mothers usually have three to five puppies in a **litter**. The mothers only carry their young for about 60 days. Westies are born blind and deaf.

Newborn puppies rely on their senses of touch and smell. They stay close to their mother's warm body. Their sense of smell helps them find their mother's milk before their eyes open. A Westie's eyes stay shut until the puppy is about two weeks old. Westies begin to hear after about three weeks.

As a small breed, Westies grow quickly. Puppies will be close to their adult height after six months.

> Liquid from a Westie puppy's eyes may stain the fur around them. Daily wiping can prevent these stains.

Westie puppies are born with small stomachs. After they stop drinking their mother's milk, they need to eat four small meals a day. Most Westies can have adult food once they are nine months old. From then on, they only need to be fed twice a day.

Young Westies must be handled with care. To pick a Westie puppy up properly, a person should put one arm between the dog's front legs and underneath the chest. The puppy should be held close to the person's body with the other arm. This helps prevent injuries.

Westies should be introduced to new people and animals when they are young. This helps them get along with people and dogs when they are older.

Westies were bred to have sturdy tails as a hunting aid. Farmers could grab the dog's tail to help pull it out of an animal's burrow.

Hard at Work

In the breed's early years, West Highland white terriers did important work on Scottish farms. The crops grown on the farms often attracted rats. These rodents would chew holes in bags of grain and storage bins to get at the food inside. Their droppings would spoil the food that they did not eat. Rats also spread numerous diseases to nearby animals and people. Farmers used Westies to control the rat population. Some were also used to hunt badgers and foxes.

The first Earthdog events were held in 1994.

Today, West Highland white terriers are still used to hunt rats both in cities and on farms. This is considered a safer form of pest control than using poison or traps. It prevents other animals, including pets, from being accidentally injured.

Some Westie owners exercise their dogs' hunting skills by taking them to events. Earthdog and Barn Hunt events were both invented in the United States and approved by the AKC. Earthdog events are typically held for fun, while Barn Hunt events are competitive and often offer prizes.

In Earthdog events, dogs must follow a scent through tunnels. Barn Hunts involve dogs finding their way to a target through an obstacle course. Often, the dogs must find animals, such as rats, that are kept in safe containers or cages.

Westies can take part in many kinds of athletic competitions. These include agility events, in which the dog travels through tunnels, over jumps, and passes other obstacles along a set course .

Taking Westies on different walking routes can help keep the dogs engaged and interested in the activity.

Caring for a Westie

West Highland white terriers can be left alone for short periods of time, but prefer to be with people. When at home with family, Westies often follow their owners around the house. They like to be in the same room as their humans and join them on walks.

When walking, Westies should always have access to fresh water, especially during hot weather. Their double coats can cause their bodies to overheat. Hot pavement or cement can also burn their paws. Cooler parts of the day are best for outdoor exercise.

Dogs with white fur are at greater risk of sunburn than other dogs. Owners should use pet sunscreen on a Westie's nose and ears.

Regular visits to the **veterinarian** are important for all dogs, including Westies. Veterinarians can help owners determine which kind of food their Westie should eat. They can also tell owners which **vaccines** the dog will need, and how to care for its teeth.

Westies often get skin **rashes**, which may cause itching and fur loss. Some rashes can be prevented by regular washing. Others might mean the dog needs a medicated shampoo. Sometimes, rashes can be caused by a food allergy, requiring a change to the dog's diet.

West Highland white terriers can live for 12 to 16 years. Some have even lived for more than 20. After 10 years, a Westie is considered a senior dog.

West Highland white terriers do not shed as much as some dogs. However, regular brushing is still recommended in order to keep the dog's coat tidy.

Westie Quiz

Q: How many puppies do most Westie mothers have?

A: Three to five

Q: Westies are known for being which color?

A: White

Q: West Highland white terriers come from which part of Great Britain?

A: Scotland

Q: Westies have a tail shaped like which vegetable?

A: A carrot

Q: What year did the AKC register the West Highland white terrier under that name?

A: 1909

Q: What is a typical Westie life span?

A: 12 to 16 years

Key Words

breeds (BREEDS): certain types of an animal

coats (KOHTS): the fur of dogs

litter (LIH-tur): a group of babies born to one animal at the same time

prey (PRAY): an animal being hunted

rashes (RA-shuhz): red areas that appear on the skin as a reaction to something

registers (REDGE-uh-sturz): puts on an official list

terriers (TER-ee-erz): small and energetic dog breeds known for their hunting skills

trait (TRAYT): a characteristic that is inherited

vaccines (vak-SEENS): medicines that help the immune system fight off specific diseases

veterinarian (veh-truh-NEH-ree-uhn): a doctor who takes care of animals

Index

Get the best of both worlds.

AV2 bridges the gap between print and digital.

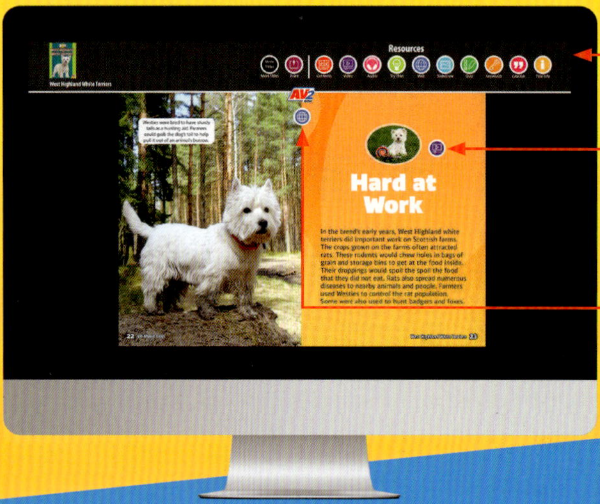

The expandable resources toolbar enables quick access to content including **videos**, **audio**, **activities**, **weblinks**, **slideshows**, **quizzes**, and **key words**.

Animated videos make static images come alive.

Resource icons on each page help readers to further **explore key concepts**.

Published by Lightbox Learning Inc.
276 5th Avenue, Suite 704 #917
New York, NY 10001
Website: www.openlightbox.com

Library of Congress Control Number: 2023008432

ISBN 978-1-7911-5642-8 (hardcover)
ISBN 978-1-7911-5643-5 (softcover)
ISBN 978-1-7911-5644-2 (multi-user eBook)

Printed in Guangzhou, China
1 2 3 4 5 6 7 8 9 0 27 26 25 24 23

042023
101322

Project Coordinator: John Willis
Designer: Terry Paulhus

Photo Credits
Every reasonable effort has been made to trace ownership and to obtain permission to reprint copyright material. The publisher would be pleased to have any errors or omissions brought to its attention so that they may be corrected in subsequent printings. The publisher acknowledges Alamy, Dreamstime, Getty Images, Newscom, and Shutterstock as its primary image suppliers for this title.